Hi, everyone.
Allow me to introduce myself.
My name is Cookie.

And this is my sister, Sugar, the quiet one.

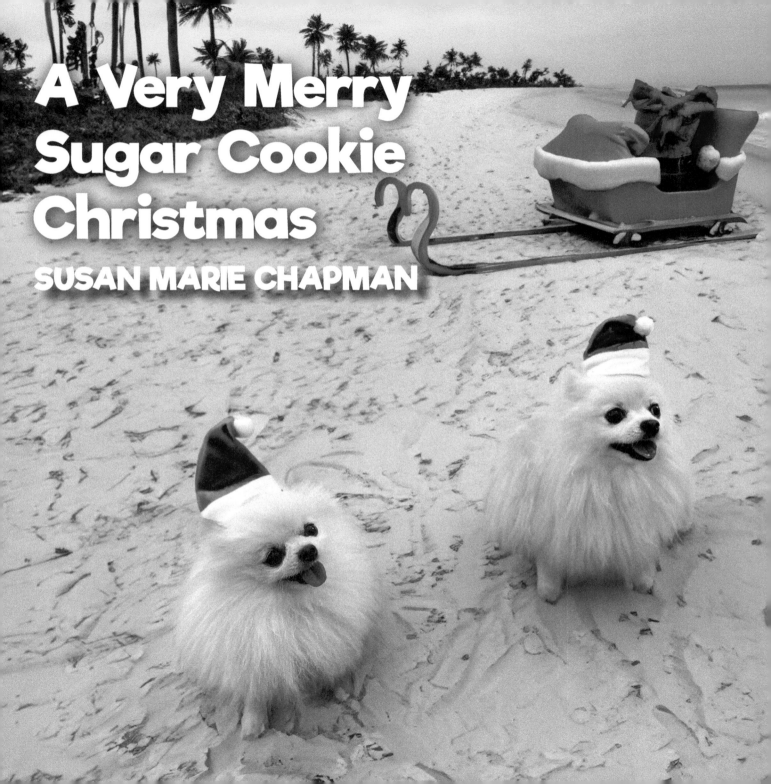

A Very Merry Sugar Cookie Christmas

SUSAN MARIE CHAPMAN

Printed in the United States of America

Hardcover ISBN: 978-1-7368056-9-5

Canoe Tree
Press

Canoe Tree Press is a division of DartFrog Books
www.DartFrogBooks.com

Special thanks to:
Seth and Maria Schiller of Design Naples Inc.
Hernan Sanchez of Stills By Hernan LLC.
Inn On Fifth for their entryway
"Everything Is Extra" Photo

We are two of the cutest and fluffiest white Pomeranians you will ever see.

July 19 is our birthday, but we did not meet our human mommy until right before Christmas in December.

That's how we came to be Sugar and Cookie.

Sugar cookies are a favorite Christmas cookie; plus, they are yummy, just like us.

We have had many nicknames over the years, such as Puffballs, Clouds with Legs, and Cotton Balls, but we will always prefer just Sugar and Cookie.

Curious minds want to know what is so special about Christmas time in Florida.

What is all the fuss about?

We have heard the whisperings
of people and their dogs asking the question.
Do Floridians even notice
that it is Christmas time?

The answer is yes,
and we Florida girls can prove it.

The excitement starts in November, right after Thanksgiving, when all the decorations go up.

There is magic in the air.

Sugar, do you see what I see?

I see Sparkle and Shine.

And fun times.

Definitely more laughing and smiling.
No grumpy faces can be found.

Everything is "extra."

People are extra helpful.
Opening doors for one another.

Holding hands.

Using their magic words, *please* and *thank you*.

Remember, Santa is watching.

Believe it or not, Florida does get cold in the winter.

Our human mom makes us wear sweaters.
(If only dogs could talk, we would say, "No sweaters, please.")

We get extra hugs and kisses during Christmas time too.

We will probably never build a snowman
or make snow angels,
nor will we ever go on a sleigh ride in Florida,
but we can certainly sit in Santa's sleigh for a photo op.

This is one of our favorite manger scenes in Florida.

Sugar and I love Christmas in Florida, and we invite you to join us so that you can feel the magic too.

Because the spirit of Christmas time is for everyone, no matter where you live.

The End

Printed in the USA
CPSIA information can be obtained
at www.ICGtesting.com
LVHW071551081123
763021LV00002B/2